This book belongs to

....

Egg Fried Rice and Other Stories

How this collection works

This *Biff, Chip and Kipper* collection is one of a series of four books at **Read with Oxford Stage 3**. It is divided into two distinct halves.

The first half focuses on phonics, with two stories written in line with the phonics your child will have learned at school: *Egg Fried Rice* and *Ice City*. The second half contains two stories that use everyday language: *Looking After Gran* and *Mountain Rescue*. These stories help to broaden your child's wider reading experience. There are also fun activities to enjoy throughout the book.

How to use this book

Find a time to read with your child when they are not too tired and are happy to concentrate for about fifteen minutes. Reading at this stage should be a shared and enjoyable experience. It is best to choose just one story for each session.

There are tips for each part of the book to help you make the most of the stories and activities. The tips for reading on pages 4 and 28 show you how to introduce your child to the phonics stories.

The tips for reading on pages 58 and 88 explain how you can best approach reading the stories that use a wider vocabulary. At the end of each of the four stories you will find four 'Talk about the story' questions. These will help your child to think about what they have read, and to relate the story to their own experiences. The questions are followed by a fun activity.

Enjoy sharing the stories!

Contents

OXFORD
UNIVERSITY PRESS

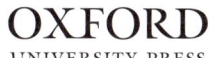

Phonics

Tips for reading *Egg Fried Rice*

Children learn best when reading is relaxed and enjoyable.

- Talk about the title and the picture on page 5, and read the speech bubble.
- Identify the letter patterns *ie*, *igh*, *i-e* and *y* in the story, and talk about the sound they make when you read them ('igh').
- Look at the *ie*, *i-e*, *igh* and *y* words on page 6. Say the sound then read the words (e.g. *igh* – *light*; *i-e* – *nice*).
- Read the story together, then find the words with *ie* and *i-e*, *igh* and *y* in them.
- Talk about the story and do the fun activities at the end of the story.

Children enjoy re-reading stories and this helps to build their confidence.

After you have read the story, see how many Chinese lanterns you can find.

The main sound practised in this story is 'igh' as in *tried*, *nine*, *night*, and *cried*.

For more activities, free eBooks and practical advice to help your child progress with reading visit **oxfordowl.co.uk**

Egg Fried Rice

Wilma has a birthday to remember!

Say the sounds and read the words

igh
- br**igh**t
- l**igh**t
- r**igh**t

ie
- fr**ie**d
- tr**ie**d
- cr**ie**d

y
- tr**y**
- sk**y**
- cr**y**

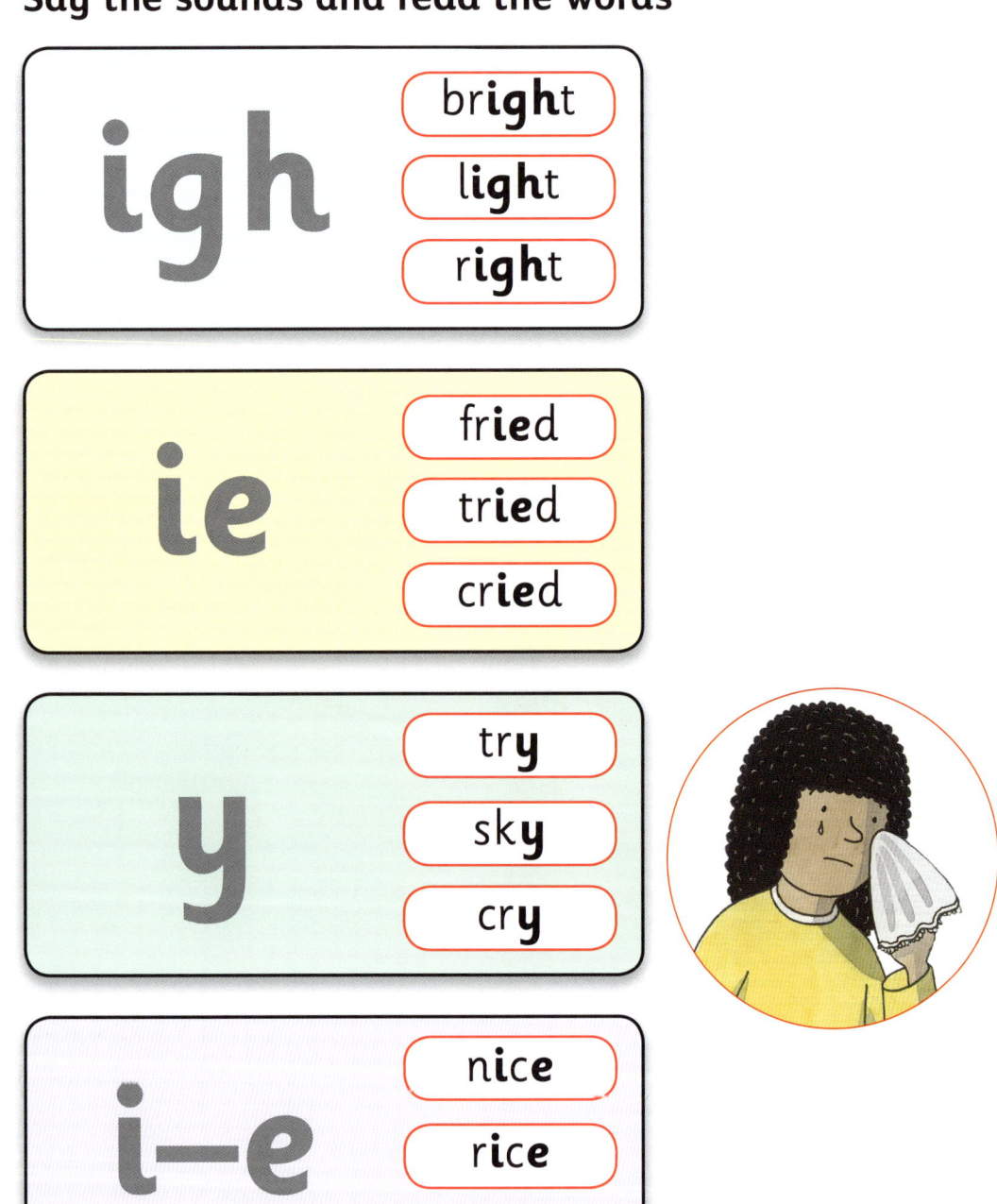

i–e
- n**i**c**e**
- r**i**c**e**
- n**i**n**e**

"I will be nine on Friday," said Wilma.
"I'd like to eat out."

"I'd like a Chinese meal," Wilma said,
"and can we invite Biff and Chip?"

"That's fine," said Mum.

It was time for the Chinese meal.
They went to the Bright Sky.

"What is it like to be nine?" said Chip.

Wilma smiled.

"It's all right," she said.

"What do you like best?" said Dad.

"I like egg fried rice," said Wilma,
"and I'll try tiger prawns."

Then all the lights went out. Oh no!
There was a fire.

"The kitchen is on fire!" said Mr Lee.

They had to go outside. Fire-fighters
came to put the fire out.

"I am sorry," said Mr Lee. "We must shut for the night."

Wilma was upset. She tried not to, but she cried.

"It is sad to see Wilma cry," said
Mr Lee. "Come back on Sunday night."

On Sunday, Mr Lee put on a feast.

"Smile," said Mr Lee.

"This is so kind," said Mum.

"I had my egg fried rice," said Wilma, "and such a nice time."

Talk about the story

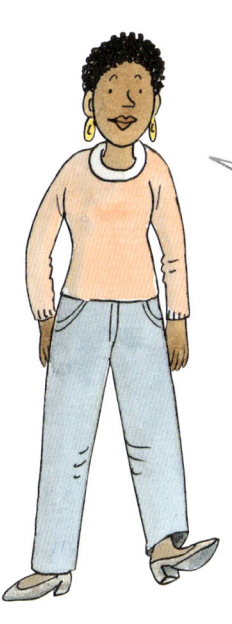

Where did the family go for their meal?

Why was Wilma upset when there was a fire?

How did Mr Lee cheer Wilma up?

What do you like to eat when you go out for a meal?

Word jumble

Make the *igh*, *ie*, *i–e* and *y* words from the story.

t	r	igh	b

n	e	f	i

s	igh	l	t

y	r	c

e	n	c	i

ie, *i-e*, *y* or *igh*?

Choose the letters to make each word.

n___t   n__n_   sm__l_

tr___d   l__k_   r___t

br___t   fr___d   cr__

Picture puzzle

Bright Sky

Find as many *igh*, *ie*, *i–e* and *y* words as you can in the picture.

igh

i-e

Tips for reading *Ice City*

Children learn best when reading is relaxed and enjoyable.

- Talk about the title and the picture on page 29, and read the speech bubble.

- Identify the letter patterns *ce* and *c* in the title and *ss* and *se* in the story, and talk about the sound they make when you read them ('s').

- Look at the *c*, *ss*, *ce* and *se* words on page 30. Say the sounds in each word and then say each word (e.g. *c-i-t-y*, *city*; *g-l-a-ss*, *glass*; *i-ce*, *ice*; *g-ee-se*, *geese*).

- Read the story together, then find the words with the letter patterns *c*, *se*, *ss* and *ce* in them.

- Talk about the story and do the fun activity at the end of the story.

Children enjoy re-reading stories and this helps to build their confidence.

Have fun!

After you have read the story, see how many different ice animals you can find.

The main sound practised in this story is 's' as in *dress*, *city*, *nurse* and *palace*.

 For more activities, free eBooks and practical advice to help your child progress with reading visit **oxfordowl.co.uk**

Ice City

The family have fun in Ice City!

Read these words

city	i**ce**
dre**ss**	prin**ce**
gla**ss**	pala**ce**
gee**se**	nur**se**

30

Mum and Dad took the children to Ice City.

"So this is Ice City," said Biff. "What a place!"

"It's all made of ice," said Chip. "This is so exciting."

They went to the Ice Palace. It had
scenes from fairy tales. They were made
out of ice.

"I can see Puss in Boots," said Kipper.

"And here is Mother Goose," said Mum.
"Look at all the geese."

"Guess who this is," said Biff. "Look
at her dress."

"See. It's Cinderella and the Ugly Sisters," said Biff.

What an ugly sister.

"The sisters were not nice to Cinderella," said Kipper.

They went skating. Kipper did not
like skating.

Oh no! Biff hit Chip in the face. It was an accident.

A nurse looked at Chip's face.

"It's fine," she said.

"We all need some dinner," said Dad.

"Let's go and eat."

They went to The Ice House.
It was made of ice.

They had a slice of pizza and
some water.

"Even my glass is made of ice,"
said Kipper.

After dinner, Dad took the children
on the bobsleigh ride.

"The bobsleigh will bump," said Dad.

The ride began.

"It's like a real bobsleigh," said Kipper.

"It's exciting!" called Biff.

"It's like a real race," said Chip.

The sun began to go down.

"Look at Ice City in the sunset," said Mum.

"It's all lit up by the sun," said Chip.

The moon rose. Ice City went silver.

"It's all lit up by the moon," said Biff.

"It looks so peaceful."

"Time for bed," said Dad.

"What a super day," said Biff.

Talk about the story

How can you tell the family is on holiday?

Which fairy tale scenes did the children spot?

Why did Biff say sorry to Chip?

What would you like to do if you visited Ice City?

Missing letters

Find the missing letters by looking back in the story.

Pu___ in boots

Mother Goo___

_inderella   the prin___

Ugly _i_ter

Stories for Wider Reading

Children learn best when reading is relaxed and enjoyable. These two stories use simple everyday language. You can help your child to read any more challenging words in the context of the story. Children enjoy re-reading stories and this helps to build their confidence and their vocabulary.

Have fun!

Tips for reading *Looking After Gran*

- Talk about the title and the picture on page 59, and read the speech bubble.
- Share the story, encouraging your child to read as much of it as they can.
- Give lots of praise as your child reads, and help them when necessary.
- If your child gets stuck on a word that is easily decodable, encourage them to say the sounds and then blend them together to read the word. Read the whole sentence again. Focus on the meaning. If the word is not decodable, or is still too tricky, just read the word for them and move on.
- When you've finished reading the story, talk about it with your child, using the 'Talk about the story' questions at the end.
- Do the activity on page 86.
- Re-read the story later, again encouraging your child to read as much of it as they can.

After you have read the story, find the 10 even numbers in the pictures.

For more activities, free eBooks and practical advice to help your child progress with reading visit **oxfordowl.co.uk**

This story includes these useful common words:

thought   must   looking   find

Looking After Gran

Floppy looks after Gran!

The family was going away.
"Look after Floppy," said Dad.

Gran liked looking after Floppy. She took him for lots of walks.

She threw sticks for him to
chase and balls for him to catch.

Gran had a motorbike. It was
bright red.

"Jump in, Floppy," said Gran.

Gran put on her crash helmet.

"Where are we going?"

thought Floppy.

Soon, they were zooming into town.
"Isn't this fun!" said Gran.

"Not for me!" thought Floppy.

At last, Gran stopped. She parked
the motorbike on the sand.

"Stay here, Floppy," said Gran.
"Look after the motorbike. I'm
going shopping."

Gran was away for a long time. The
tide started to come in. A wave
splashed the front wheel.

Then a wave splashed the back wheel.

"Gran has parked too close to the sea!" thought Floppy.

"I must find Gran," thought Floppy.

He ran into the town as fast as
he could.

Sniff! Sniff! went Floppy.

He could tell where Gran had been.

She had been in the butcher's shop.

"Yum! Bones," thought Floppy.

"Get out!" yelled the butcher. "No dogs in here!"

Floppy ran back into
the street.

"I must find Gran," he
thought.

Sniff! Sniff! went Floppy.

Gran had been in the bread shop.

"Get out!" yelled the baker. "No dogs in here!"

Floppy ran back into
the street.
"I must find Gran,"
he thought.

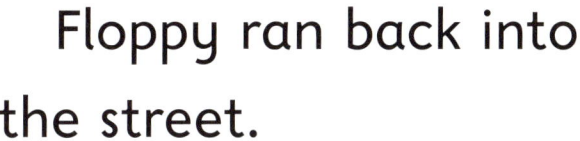

Then Floppy saw Gran. She was
in the hat shop. Floppy ran in and
barked.

"Get out!" said the lady. "No dogs
in here!"

"Come on, Gran!" thought Floppy.

Floppy ran out of the shop. Gran ran after him.

"Come back!" called the lady. "You haven't paid for that hat."

Floppy ran
back to the beach.
Gran puffed
after him.

"Oh no! My motorbike,"
shouted Gran.

She ran into the sea and pushed her
motorbike out.

"Well done, Floppy," said Gran. "You saved my motorbike!"

Gran spoke to Mum.

"I'm not looking after Floppy," she said. "He's looking after me!"

Talk about the story

Why didn't Floppy like going on Gran's motorbike?

Why did Gran leave Floppy with her motorbike?

Gran told Floppy to stay. Why was he right not to stay?

What animal would you like to look after for a day?

Spot the difference

Find the ten differences between the motorbikes.

Tips for reading *Mountain Rescue*

Children learn best when reading is relaxed and enjoyable.

- Talk about the title and the picture on page 89, and read the speech bubble.

- Share the story, encouraging your child to read as much of it as they can with you.

- Give lots of praise as your child reads, and help them when necessary.

- If your child gets stuck on a word that is easily decodable, encourage them to say the sounds and then blend them together to read the word. Read the whole sentence again. Focus on the meaning. If the word is not decodable, or is still too tricky, just read the word for them and move on.

- When you've finished reading the story, talk about it with your child, using the 'Talk about the story' questions at the end.

- Do the activity on page 116.

- Re-read the story later, again encouraging your child to read as much of it as they can.

After you have read the story, find the 10 hiking boots hidden in the pictures.

Have fun!

This story includes these useful common words:
suddenly   shouted   station
climbed/climbing/climber

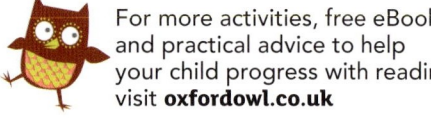

For more activities, free eBooks and practical advice to help your child progress with reading visit **oxfordowl.co.uk**

Mountain Rescue

What do Biff and Wilma rescue?

Biff was showing Wilma her new music box.

"It's like a little house," said Wilma.

Biff opened the box and the music
began to play. Suddenly, the magic
key began to glow.

The magic took Biff and Wilma to a mountain railway station.

"The station looks just like my music box," said Biff.

There was a big wooden horn at the station. A boy called Max told them that it was used to send for the Mountain Rescue helicopter.

"My Uncle Hans flies the helicopter," he said. "He's taking me to see an eagle's nest today. You can come with us."

The children got into a train. It took them higher up the mountain. Uncle Hans was waiting at the station.

"Hi Max," said Uncle Hans. "I'm glad
some of your friends have come
with you."

Uncle Hans and the children went up a steep track. They saw some people climbing a steep rock.

"That looks scary!" said Biff.

Just then, Uncle Hans's phone rang.
"I have to go back, but you can see
the eagle's nest from here," he said.

The eagle was sitting on her nest.
Suddenly, she squawked and flew into
the sky.

"A man has climbed up to the nest!" said Biff. "He's putting the eagle's egg into his bag."

"Put that egg back!" shouted Wilma. The man looked up. He saw the children watching him and started to run.

"He's going to the station," said Max. "Quick! Let's follow him and get the egg back." They slipped and scrambled down the steep path.

At last, they reached the station.
Wilma ran up to the man.

"We saw you take an egg from the
eagle's nest," she said.

The man was angry. "I didn't take an egg," he said, and he opened his bag. There was no egg inside.

Suddenly, there was a shout.

"One of the climbers has fallen!"
said Max. "We must call the Mountain
Rescue Team."

Wilma ran to blow the horn, but the man tried to stop her.

"Give me that horn!" he shouted, but Wilma pulled it away from him.

Wilma looked in the horn. "He's
hidden the egg in here!" she said.

The man started to run but Biff
tripped him up . . . CRASH!

Max took the egg and wrapped it in his jacket to keep it warm.

Then Wilma blew the horn.

BOOM! . . . BOOM! . . . BOOM!

The Mountain Rescue helicopter
flew into the sky. Everyone cheered
as the climber was lifted to safety.

The helicopter landed and Max
showed Uncle Hans the eagle's egg.

"We must put the egg back before it
gets cold," said Uncle Hans.

Uncle Hans climbed up to the nest and put the egg back. The eagle saw the egg and flew back to her nest.

Three big feathers floated gently
down to the children.

"The eagle is saying thank you," said
Biff, as the magic key glowed.

"Look! There's a wooden horn on your music box now," said Wilma. "How did it get there?"

"It must be magic," smiled Biff.

Talk about the story

What was the big wooden horn used for?

How do you think the children felt when the man showed them his empty bag?

Why did Max wrap the egg in his jacket?

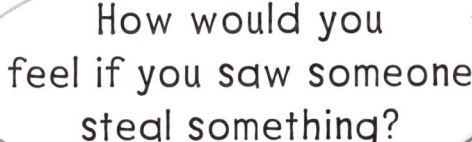

How would you feel if you saw someone steal something?

A maze

Help Uncle Hans put the egg back.

Remembering the stories together

Encourage your child to remember and retell the stories in this book.
You could ask questions like these:

- Who are the characters?
- What happens at the beginning?
- What happens next?
- How does the story end?
- What was your favourite part? Why?

Story prompts

When talking to your child about the stories, you could use these more detailed reminders to help them remember the exact sequence of events. Turn the statements below into questions, so that your child can give you the answers. For example, *Where does Wilma go for her birthday? Why did the lights go out?* And so on …

Egg Fried Rice

- Wilma goes to a Chinese restaurant for her birthday.
- As they are about to order, all the lights go out because the kitchen is on fire!
- Firefighters put out the fire, but the restaurant has to shut for the night.
- Mr Lee invites them to come back another night.
- He puts a feast on for them.

Ice City

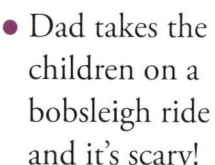

- Mum and Dad take the children to Ice City.
- They see Puss in Boots and Cinderella made out of ice.
- Kipper doesn't like ice-skating.
- Biff hits Chip in the face by accident.
- Dad takes the children on a bobsleigh ride and it's scary!
- They have a great day.

Looking after Gran

- Gran is looking after Floppy.
- She takes Floppy for a ride on her motorbike.
- Floppy doesn't enjoy being on the motorbike.
- Gran goes shopping, but parks her motorbike too close to the sea!

- Floppy goes into town to find Gran.
- Gran gets back to the beach just in time to rescue her motorbike.

Mountain Rescue

- The magic key takes Biff and Wilma to a mountain railway station.
- The children go on a train up the mountain.
- They see a man stealing an eagle's egg.
- The children catch him, but the egg isn't in his bag.

- A rock climber slips and needs rescuing.
- Wilma finds the egg hidden in the horn!

You could now encourage your child to create a 'story map' of each story, drawing and colouring all the key parts of them. This will help them to identify the main elements of the stories and learn to create their own stories.

Authors and illustrators

Egg Fried Rice written by Roderick Hunt, illustrated by Nick Schon
Ice City written by Roderick Hunt, illustrated by Alex Brychta
Looking after Gran written by Roderick Hunt, illustrated by Alex Brychta
Mountain Rescue written by Cynthia Rider, illustrated by Alex Brychta

OXFORD
UNIVERSITY PRESS

Great Clarendon Street, Oxford, OX2 6DP, United Kingdom

Oxford University Press is a department of the University
of Oxford. It furthers the University's objective of excellence
in research, scholarship, and education by publishing
worldwide. Oxford is a registered trade mark of Oxford
University Press in the UK and in certain other countries

Looking After Gran first published in 2005
Mountain Rescue first published in 2006
Ice City, *Egg Fried Rice* first published in 2008

This Edition published in 2018

British Library Cataloguing in Publication Data
Data available

ISBN: 978-0-19-276424-9

10 9 8 7 6 5 4 3 2

Paper used in the production of this book is a natural, recyclable product
made from wood grown in sustainable forests. The manufacturing process
conforms to the environmental regulations of the country of origin.

Printed in Great Britain by Bell and Bain Ltd, Glasgow

Acknowledgements

Series Editors: Annemarie Young and Kate Ruttle